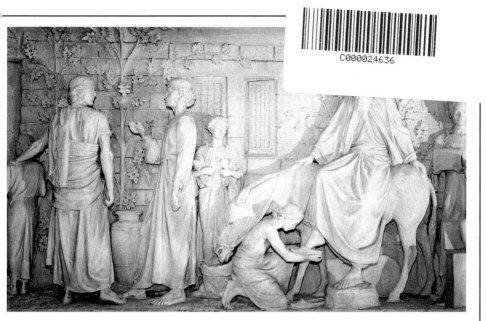

Detail of the terracotta reredos made by Doulton in St Mark's church, Shelton, Stoke-on-Trent, modelled by George Tinworth in 1902. It represents 'The Wise Men Opening Their Treasures'.

Architectural Ceramics

Hans van Lemmen

Published by Shire Publications Ltd,
Midland House, West Way, Botley, Oxford OX2 0PH, UK.
(Website: www.shirebooks.co.uk)

Copyright © 2002 by Hans van Lemmen.
First published 2002.
Transferred to digital print on demand 2011.
Shire Library 395. ISBN 978 0 74780 517 5.
Hans van Lemmen is hereby identified as the author of
this work in accordance with Section 77 of the Copyright,
Designs and Patents Act 1988.

British Library Cataloguing in Publication Data:
Van Lemmen, Hans
Architectural ceramics. – (A Shire album; 395)
1. Architecture – Great Britain – Details –
History – 19th century
2. Architecture – Great Britain – Details –
History – 20th century
3. Ceramic industries – Great Britain –
History – 19th century
4. Ceramic industries – Great Britain –
History – 20th century
I. Title 721'.0941
ISBN-10 0 7478 0517 2
ISBN-13 978 0 74780 517 5

Cover: A faience panel made by Burmantofts on the exterior of the Midland Hotel in Manchester built between 1899 and 1903. It was modelled by E. Spruce and shows the muse of sculpture.

ACKNOWLEDGEMENTS
The author is grateful to Dr Richard Tyler for reading and commenting on the
manuscript; and to Chris Blanchett, Myra Brown, Richard Dennis, Tony Herbert, Debbie
Skinner, Lynn Pearson, Jon Wilson (Shaws of Darwen), Julie Gillam Wood, Alan Swale, the
Board of Trustees of the National Museums and Galleries on Merseyside (Walker Art
Gallery), and the Gladstone Pottery Museum, Longton, Stoke-on-Trent. Illustrations are
acknowledged as follows: Walker Art Gallery, page 27 (bottom left); Gladstone Pottery
Museum, pages 7 and 26 (top); Shaws of Darwen, pages 8 and 9; Lynn Pearson, pages 11
(bottom left) and 31 (top); Tony Herbert, page 36 (bottom). All other photographs are from
the author's collection.

Printed in Great Britain by PrintOnDemand-Worldwide.com, Peterborough, UK.

Contents

A faience plaque depicting a foundling on the exterior of the Westminster Children's Hospital, Westminster, London, made by Doulton c.1930. It is based on one of the fifteenth-century faience roundels made by the Della Robbia workshop for the Foundling Hospital in Florence, Italy.

A decorative panel made by the firm of J. C. Edwards on the exterior of the Liberal Club in Leeds (1890). It is made of red unglazed terracotta and consists of several sections, which would have been assembled on site. There is evidence of undercutting and hand-finishing, which would have been done at the factory after the clay panels came out of the moulds.

Introduction

Architectural ceramics is a broad term that covers all building materials made from fired clay. It can apply to anything from bricks, chimney pots, roof tiles, wall tiles and floor tiles to complete terracotta and faience wall coverings. However, within the scope of this book it refers mainly to functional and ornamental terracotta and faience cladding for the exterior and interior of buildings.

The terms *terracotta* and *faience* can be used to indicate whether the material is unglazed or glazed. *Terracotta* (Italian for 'baked earth') is used to refer to unglazed architectural ceramics usually made in either red or buff. *Faience* (from the Italian town Faenza, a major centre for glazed-pottery production) indicates architectural ceramics covered with monochrome or polychrome glazes. These two terms can therefore be used to create a workable distinction between two different types of architectural ceramics. As always, however, there are exceptions to the rule. It is also possible to make terracotta coated with a thin transparent glaze. Although its glazed status would make it technically a faience material, the colour of the clay can still be seen so clearly through the transparent glaze that it is hard to divorce it from the class of terracotta. In faience proper, the glaze hides the colour of the clay and it is the colour of the glaze that dominates the appearance of this type of architectural ceramics. Terracotta or faience material used as a covering on the outside or inside of buildings is different from bricks and tiles. Bricks are integral to the building. Tiles, in the form of roof, wall or floor tiles, are usually flat pieces of glazed or unglazed clay; they are laid on the roof or cemented to the floor or the wall as a kind of appliqué, which can be taken off and replaced with new tiles when necessary. This is in contrast with terracotta and faience wall cladding, which is usually made in the form of substantial three-dimensional hollow blocks. They not only cover the walls, but the material can also be used (like bricks) to form window frames, door jambs and arches. The exterior of these blocks can be plain and flat, but it can also be given a decorative surface or moulded into complex three-dimensional shapes. It is ideally suited for adding sculptural embellishments to buildings when rich decorative effects are required. Terracotta and faience are, therefore, two types of extremely flexible and versatile building materials and can be used both structurally and decoratively. This double role lies behind their rise in the modern world.

Since antiquity, building material made from fired clay has been appreciated for its waterproof, fireproof, hygienic and decorative qualities. The history of architectural ceramics goes back to the Egyptians, who applied glazed tiles in their tombs and palaces. The Babylonians used colourful glazed bricks in their monumental architecture and the Greeks applied terracotta roof tiles and ornaments to their temples. The Etruscans used terracotta for funerary

Detail of the terracotta exterior of the County Arcade in Leeds (1900). The buff terracotta made by Burmantofts has been given a very thin coat of transparent glaze to make it more impervious.

A faience panel made by Burmantofts with a brown monochrome glaze, on the exterior of the Midland Hotel in Manchester, constructed between 1899 and 1903. It was modelled by E. C. Spruce and shows the muse of painting.

sculpture, while the Romans used clay tiles not only on roofs, but also on floors and in their baths. In the Middle Ages little use of architectural ceramics was made, but there was a strong revival during the Italian Renaissance. During the fifteenth and sixteenth centuries terracotta and faience were used in various types of Italian civic and religious architecture. Some of the most outstanding products were made by the fifteenth-century Della Robbia workshop in Florence, which specialised in polychrome glazed relief sculpture.

A faience roundel on the exterior of the Sunlight Chambers in Dublin made by the Medmenham Pottery in 1901. A number of coloured glazes have been used in addition to an opaque white glaze.

A late-Victorian plaster model with cupids at the Gladstone Pottery Museum in Stoke-on-Trent. The terracotta figures derived from it would have been used as part of an architectural frieze.

It was not until the emergence of a consumer society during the second half of the eighteenth century that terracotta and later faience began to find widespread applications in all kinds of domestic, civic, religious, commercial and public buildings. The Georgians, Victorians and Edwardians loved decoration, which meant that terracotta and faience ornament became a much-used building accessory. After the First World War architectural styles changed and, although the popularity of terracotta and faience declined during the inter-war period, faience was still used for certain types of buildings like cinemas, factories, department stores and housing estates. After the Second World War their popularity fell into decline even further when concrete, steel and glass became the preferred building materials. However, there was a revival towards the end of the twentieth century, with new demands for architectural ceramics in the restoration of buildings and for incorporation into post-modern architecture.

The production processes of terracotta and faience have changed much less over time than the production process of tiles. The latter is now in some instances a fully automated machine process, but handwork rather than machine work is still the norm in the making of terracotta and faience. The process begins with an architect preparing detailed drawings. At the factory, the architect's drawings are used to make working drawings for the modeller. These working drawings must take account of the shrinkage rates of the clay. A model made from plaster or clay is then made on the

A clay model of a capital in preparation at Shaws of Darwen. When finished, a model will be made from it in plaster and, from this, plaster working moulds will be made. Only at this point can the actual production of terracotta capitals begin.

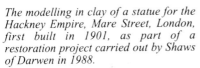

The modelling in clay of a statue for the Hackney Empire, Mare Street, London, first built in 1901, as part of a restoration project carried out by Shaws of Darwen in 1988.

basis of the working drawing: in the case of simple building components, a model can be cut directly from a plaster block; in the case of more complex sculptural ornament, the model is first made from clay and then made into a plaster model. A plaster mould in reverse, called a working mould, is then made from the plaster model, and this will be used for the manufacture of the terracotta or faience piece. Clay is pressed by hand to a thickness of about $1^{1}/4$ inches (just over 3 cm) to the inside of the mould. Once the mould is filled it is set aside for the clay to dry. The plaster will absorb moisture from the clay and when sufficiently dry the clay is separated from the mould. More complex pieces will need a certain amount of hand-finishing, or even further modelling in the case of ornate sculptural pieces. Although the process is still a hand craft, the use of moulds makes multiple production possible and thus reduces costs.

After further drying the pieces are fired in a kiln. Unglazed terracotta goes straight into the kiln and is fired at temperatures up to 1250°C. Such high temperatures ensure that the clay becomes hard and dense and therefore water- and frost-resistant. In the case of faience, a high-temperature glaze can be applied to the unfired clay and fired in one

A hand-pressed hollow architectural moulding being finished by hand at Shaws of Darwen prior to drying and firing.

A workman at Shaws of Darwen presses clay inside a circular plaster mould to make a terracotta column for restoration work at the Natural History Museum in London.

operation, again up to 1250°C. The glaze fuses tightly to the clay body, resulting in faience material that is not only frostproof but is also able to resist atmospheric pollution. Some pieces can be fired first and then glazed and fired for a second time. This procedure is sometimes used with complex pieces that are to be painted with many different-coloured glazes, which may need to be fired at a lower temperature of not more than 1050°C. Terracotta and faience blocks usually carry sequential numbers to assist their correct assembly on the building site. As the blocks are hollow they are filled with cement or concrete so that, once they have been installed, they become an integral part of the wall.

An early-sixteenth-century terracotta bust of the Roman Emperor Tiberius on the façade of Hampton Court. It was made by the Italian Giovanni da Maiano for Henry VIII.

Emergence

An early instance of the use of architectural ceramics in Britain can be found at the beginning of the sixteenth century, when there was a short-lived fashion for terracotta during the reign of Henry VIII. He employed foreign craftsmen including the Italian Giovanni da Maiano, who came from Florence, where there was a well-established tradition of architectural terracotta and faience. Maiano made some fine terracotta roundels showing Roman emperors, which still decorate the exterior of Hampton Court Palace. The vogue for Renaissance-style terracotta decorations spread to other great Tudor houses, such as Sutton Place in Surrey, Layer Marney in Essex, and East Barsham Hall in Norfolk. The demise of Italian-inspired terracotta on early Tudor houses was probably due to the break with Rome instigated by Henry VIII and the subsequent English Reformation. It would not be until the eighteenth century that a renewed interest in the use of architectural terracotta was evident.

A key figure in this story is Eleanor Coade (1733–1821), who established a terracotta factory at Lambeth, London, in

1769. Like other ceramic entrepreneurs (for example, Wedgwood) she was responding to the period's rising consumer demands. The prevailing neo-classical style of architecture in the eighteenth century meant a demand for all manner of classical decoration in the form of ornamental capitals for columns, balusters, keystones, chimney stacks, friezes, medallions and plaques, as well as garden sculpture, gateways, sundials, urns and vases. Replicating these items in stone was expensive so a grey-coloured terracotta closely resembling stone was the answer for the new market. In fact, Mrs Coade's products were marketed as 'artificial stone' and in her factory all kinds of architectural ornament and sculpture were made with the aid of plaster moulds. Well-known architects of the day, such as Robert Adam, Samuel Wyatt and John Nash, made use of Coade-stone products. Since terracotta products were closely associated with brickmaking, terracotta may have been marketed as 'artificial stone' in order to avoid brick tax, which was levied between 1784 and 1850.

Above: The top sections of a doorway in Bedford Square, London, showing a Coade-stone keystone with a classical head and rusticated voussoirs, c.1775.

Terracotta masquerading as stone not only was used in secular architecture but also found application in churches. One example is St Pancras church, London, consecrated in

Below left: A Coade-stone lion modelled by William Woodington in 1837. It once graced the top of the Lion Brewery in London but has now found a new home on Westminster Bridge.

Left: One of the terracotta Caryatids in the north portico of St Pancras church, London, built 1818–22. They were made to resemble stone and were modelled by John Rossi, who until 1814 had worked at the Coade factory in London.

11

Left: An engraving of a pinnacle made of white terracotta by Henry Blanchard for the Great Exhibition, as illustrated in 'The Industry of All Nations 1851 – The Art Journal Illustrated Catalogue'.

1822. William Inwood designed it in a Greek Revival style inspired by an Ionic temple, the Erectheion on the Acropolis in Athens. The church was built in brick faced with Portland stone. It has two porticoes with terracotta decorations projecting from the north and south sides. They are embellished with striking Greek female figures known as Caryatids. These load-bearing columns in the shape of Greek women were manufactured from grey-coloured terracotta. They were made by John Rossi, who until 1814 had worked for Coade.

After Mrs Coade's death in 1821, the manufacture of Coade stone continued under the direction of William Croggon. However, production ceased in 1838 and the moulds and equipment were sold off. Two individuals who bought moulds were Mark Henry Blanchard and John Blashfield. Blanchard had previously worked at the Coade factory and founded his own firm in 1839. He made terracotta garden ornaments and some architectural components, some of which were exhibited at the Great Exhibition of 1851. Blashfield was initially a cement and scagliola (artificial marble) manufacturer but he began to experiment with terracotta production in the 1840s. He began the production of terracotta in earnest after having seen terracotta work at the Great Exhibition.

There were also interesting experiments with the use of terracotta in places other than London. Examples can be

Tudor-style terracotta chimney pots manufactured by Doulton for the Great Exhibition, as illustrated in 'The Industry of All Nations 1851 – The Art Journal Illustrated Catalogue'.

St Stephen and All Martyrs' church (1842–5), Lever Bridge, Bolton, designed by the architect Edmund Sharpe. At first glance it looks like a stone church, but it has been completely constructed of terracotta made by John Fletcher.

found in Shropshire and Lancashire, where architects such as Thomas Penson and Edmund Sharpe used terracotta in the construction of Gothic Revival churches, which became known as 'pot' churches. One example of particular interest is the church of St Stephen and All Martyrs at Lever Bridge, Bolton, Lancashire. The church was designed by Edmund Sharpe and built between 1842 and 1845. A local man, John Fletcher, who had discovered suitable clay near his colliery, made the terracotta for the church. Not only was terracotta used to construct the whole fabric of the church, but it was also used for the pews and the organ case, proving that it could be both structural and decorative. Yet the use of terracotta for churches did not meet with a favourable response from the church establishment and most church architects remained faithful to the well-proven use of stone.

During the second half of the eighteenth century and the first half of the nineteenth century, terracotta had been used mainly on a small scale as a cheaper substitute for stone. It was not until the second half of the nineteenth century that it came to be valued as a material in its own right and used as an equal or sometimes superior alternative to stone.

St Stephen and All Martyrs' church (1842–5), Lever Bridge, Bolton. The pew ends and backs are entirely made of terracotta. The ceramic artist Diana Hall has been involved in the restoration of some of the poppyheads.

Heyday

The Great Exhibition of 1851 had made many people more aware of the need to improve the quality of industrial design. Several designers, architects and arts administrators, among them Richard Redgrave, Owen Jones and Henry Cole, attempted to do so. Henry Cole in particular played an important part in this quest. In 1849 he founded the *Journal of Design*, and he played a leading role in the organisation of the Great Exhibition. He was one of the first directors of the South Kensington Museum (now the Victoria and Albert Museum) and in this capacity he was involved in new buildings for the museum.

Cole's travels in Italy in 1858 acquainted him with the use of terracotta and faience in Renaissance buildings and as a consequence he encouraged its use in the construction of the South Kensington Museum during the 1860s. The quadrangle and some of the internal rooms and staircases are richly decorated with terracotta and faience designed by such artists as Godfrey Sykes and Frank Moody. A number of different manufacturers were involved in this prestige project: Blanchard, Doulton, Gibbs & Canning, Maw & Company, and Minton, Hollins &

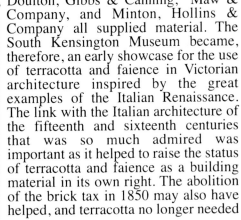

Company all supplied material. The South Kensington Museum became, therefore, an early showcase for the use of terracotta and faience in Victorian architecture inspired by the great examples of the Italian Renaissance. The link with the Italian architecture of the fifteenth and sixteenth centuries that was so much admired was important as it helped to raise the status of terracotta and faience as a building material in its own right. The abolition of the brick tax in 1850 may also have helped, and terracotta no longer needed

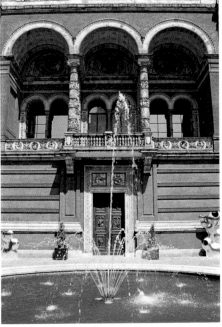

The south façade of the lecture-theatre block in the quadrangle of the Victoria and Albert Museum, London. It was built in 1864–8 according to designs by Francis Fowke and Godfrey Sykes and extensively decorated with terracotta made by several firms such as Henry Blanchard, Doulton and Minton, Hollins & Company. The columns on the balcony, showing the 'Ages of Man' by the artist Godfrey Sykes, are particularly noteworthy.

A terracotta block with a cupid on the façade of the official residence at the Victoria and Albert Museum (1862–3). It was modelled by Godfrey Sykes and made by Henry Blanchard.

the earlier guise of 'artificial stone' but could now be openly marketed for what it was.

But there are other buildings in South Kensington which show the early use of terracotta. The Albert Hall designed by H. Scott and R. Townroe between 1867 and 1871 is built of red brick embellished with buff terracotta made by Gibbs & Canning. The architects, who drew their inspiration for the design from Roman amphitheatres, used terracotta for all the cornices, balustrades and window and door jambs.

Early showpieces of the use of terracotta in architecture in the Victorian period can be found not only in London. In the heart of the pottery-making area of Staffordshire, the

Below left: Detail of the faience decorations on the ceramic staircase at the Victoria and Albert Museum (1865–71). They were designed by Frank Moody and made by a number of firms such as Maw & Company, Gibbs & Canning, and Minton, Hollins & Company.

Below right: Cupids designed by James Gamble for a column made of polychrome faience in the former refreshment room at the Victoria and Albert Museum. Minton, Hollins & Company made the faience tiles for this project, which was finished in 1868.

The Albert Hall, London, was designed by H. Scott and R. Townroe in 1867–71 and decorated with terracotta in a classical style made by Gibbs & Canning.

Wedgwood Institute in Burslem, Stoke-on-Trent, was built between 1863 and 1873. Like the South Kensington Museum, the Wedgwood Institute was designed as an educational complex consisting of a museum, library and classrooms, and it was meant to be a showcase for the rich possibilities of terracotta as a building material on a par with stone. The architect Robert Edgar designed an ornate Italian-Gothic façade constructed of brick, tiles and terracotta. A fully round terracotta sculpture of Wedgwood made by Rowland Morris stands above the entrance, flanked on both sides by terracotta panels showing the months of the year, also designed and modelled by Rowland Morris. In addition there are several panels illustrating the processes of pottery manufacture; Matthew Elden designed them and Rowland Morris was again the modeller. All the modelling

The Wedgwood Institute, Burslem, Staffordshire, built 1863–73, was a showcase for the use of terracotta. It has terracotta decorations in the form of a statue of Josiah Wedgwood, panels of the months of the year, and panels showing the manufacturing processes of pottery.

16

Above: One of the 'processes' panels on the Wedgwood Institute showing the making of vases. It was designed by Matthew Elden, modelled by Rowland Morris and fired at Blashfield's factory in Stamford, Lincolnshire. The panels were produced between 1867 and 1871.

Right: One of the 'months' panels on the Wedgwood Institute. Showing May, it was designed and modelled by Rowland Morris and fired at Blanchard's factory in London. Like the processes panels, they were produced over a period of some years, between 1867 and 1872.

work was done at the South Kensington School of Art in London. The clay and material for the month panels were supplied by the firm of Blanchard, which upon their completion also fired them. The firm of Blashfield did likewise for the process panels. The whole undertaking was therefore a complex co-operative venture involving many people – which may be the reason why it took ten years to complete.

The most significant terracotta building of the period is without doubt the Natural History Museum in South Kensington, London, designed by Alfred Waterhouse and built between 1873 and 1881. He chose to design the façade in a Romanesque style, moving away from the two dominant Victorian architectural styles, the Classical and the Gothic. The massive and bold façade is constructed entirely of buff and blue-grey terracotta blocks manufactured by Gibbs & Canning. If the South Kensington Museum, the Albert Hall and the Wedgwood Institute emphasise the decorative and sculptural potential of terracotta, the Natural History Museum shows how terracotta can be used both for complete construction and

for ornament. One of the attractive features is the fascinating range of sculptures of extinct and living animals. Pterodactyls, sabre-tooth tigers, lizards, lions, snakes and birds adorn the building in great profusion, not only marking the identity of the museum but also presenting the visitor with a lesson in zoology eternalised in terracotta.

From 1870 onwards the use of terracotta as a building material suitable for both construction and decoration increased rapidly throughout Britain. A number of factors contributed. New materials were developed and new uses were found in an enormous range of public, commercial and private buildings. Perhaps most important was the Victorian love of ornament. This was expressed in a proliferation of styles, not only revivals (of Roman, the Romanesque, the Gothic, the Renaissance), but also new developments like Arts and Crafts and Art Nouveau. If firms like Blanchard, Blashfield and Gibbs & Canning had dominated the early scene, it was now the turn of manufacturers such as Doulton, Burmantofts and J. C. Edwards to rise to prominence and supply an ever-growing market with a great variety of terracotta and faience products.

Doulton made important contributions to the development of Victorian terracotta and faience with the introduction of

Detail of the entrance of St Pauls House, Park Square, Leeds, designed by T. Ambler in a Venetian-Moorish style in 1878. The Doulton terracotta is complemented with glazed stoneware tiles.

new materials. By the 1870s Doulton was producing good-quality terracotta, which was fired to a high temperature to make it impervious to attacks by damp and frost. Its matt-coloured faience was sometimes used in combination with salt-glazed stoneware, known as Doultonware, of which the entrance of St Pauls House (1878) in Leeds is still a splendid example. Salt-glazed Doultonware was also used to decorate the lavish entrance of the Palsgrove Hotel (1883), now Lloyds TSB Bank, in London. Here glazed Doultonware is used in combination with special unglazed terracotta mosaic tiles known as Siliconware.

If salt-glazed Doultonware had proved successful in resisting the effects of damp, frost and smoke polluted with soot and acid, its glossy surface was regarded as a less desirable element. In the mid 1880s Doulton launched a new type of faience called Carraraware, which not only could resist the elements and atmospheric pollution, but also had a matt surface to counteract the intrusive effects of light reflections. Asia House in Lime Street, London, is an example of white Carraraware. Although much Carraraware was made with a durable off-white glaze, it could in effect be made in any colour. In the space of ten years Doulton had greatly advanced the technology of terracotta and faience production to meet various technical and aesthetic requirements.

Doulton also moved ahead in the artistic field because it engaged artists of the highest quality to work with terracotta and faience. Two artists of note are George Tinworth and

The ornate and somewhat exotic entrance of the former Palsgrove Hotel (now Lloyds TSB Bank), Fleet Street, London (1883). It is entirely faced with glazed Doultonware.

Left: The terracotta tympanum over the entrance of the former Doulton offices, High Street, Lambeth, London. The figures were modelled by George Tinworth in 1876. It shows Henry Doulton in the centre surrounded by his modellers and artists, one of whom, Hannah Barlow, can be seen sitting on a chair decorating a vase.

Right: The vestibule of Alexandra House, South Kensington, London, designed by C. P. Clarke (1884–7). It is decorated with green Doulton faience in a Jacobean style.

Below: The terracotta panel made by Doulton in the entrance of Alexandra House, South Kensington, London (1884–7). The figure represents Art and was designed by R. A. Ledward.

William J. Neatby. George Tinworth, an exponent of Victorian naturalism, began to work for Doulton in 1867 and soon made his name as an outstanding modeller. Much of his early work was in the field of salt-glazed stoneware, of which his fountain for the 1878 Paris Exhibition is still a *tour de force*. It showed many intricately modelled figures representing incidents from the Bible in which water was involved. Tinworth made his name, however, with highly modelled terracotta panels showing Biblical scenes. These were used in many churches throughout Britain as part of altar decorations or in pulpits. Examples can still be seen at York Minster (1876) and at St Mark's church (1896–1902), Shelton, Stoke-on-Trent.

William J. Neatby began his career with Burmantofts in Leeds in the late 1880s before joining Doulton in 1890, becoming a technical manager in the architectural

Right: Detail of the salt-glazed stoneware fountain made by Doulton for the 1878 Paris Exhibition. The figures were modelled by George Tinworth and represent scenes from the Bible associated with water. Shown here is the miracle of Jesus turning water into wine.

Below: Detail of the façade of the Everard Building, Broad Street, Bristol (1901). William J. Neatby designed the Art Nouveau decorations made in coloured Carraraware by Doulton.

Above: Detail of the Doulton faience decorations on the exterior of the Outpatients Department of the Royal Hospital for Women and Children, Waterloo Road, London (1903–5). The figure of the woman with flowing hair is reminiscent of the Art Nouveau movement.

department. His style of design was very different from the naturalism of Tinworth. Neatby's work is more decorative and closely linked to the Art Nouveau style, which was popular around 1900. This can be seen in the polychrome exterior of the Everard Building (1901) in Bristol, with images celebrating the printer's craft. His best work is in the colourful ceramic interior of Harrods Meat Hall (1902), which to this day is still one of the most opulent Art Nouveau interiors in Britain.

Between 1880 and 1914 Burmantofts in Leeds was a major producer of terracotta and faience for interior and exterior use and examples of its work can be seen in most

A corner of the sumptuous bathroom at Gledhow Hall, Leeds, decorated with Burmantofts tiles and faience (1885).

major cities throughout Britain. One of its specialities was the complete ceramic interior, where not only the walls were covered with faience, but the ceiling as well. The architect Maurice B. Adams undertook architectural designs, and sculptors such as E. Caldwell Spruce did modelling work for the firm. In 1889 Burmantofts amalgamated with other Yorkshire firms and became the Leeds Fireclay Company, but this continued to use the by now well-known trade name Burmantofts. Its products were used widely in hotels, restaurants, railway stations, shopping arcades, college buildings, banks, hospitals and domestic interiors. The corridors of the West Riding Pauper and Lunatic Asylum (now High Royds Hospital) at Menston, West Yorkshire (1888), the refreshment rooms at Newcastle station (1892), the County Arcades (1900) in Leeds, and the Midland Hotel

Above: The ceramic ceiling made of Burmantofts faience in the basement bar of the Royal York Hotel, York (c.1885).

Ornate faience columns made by Burmantofts in the refreshment rooms at the railway station, Newcastle upon Tyne (1892).

(1899–1903) in Manchester are some examples of its work.

Another major firm was J. C. Edwards in Ruabon, Wales. The fireclays mined in the area produce a strong pink-red colour when burnt, and this was one of the major characteristics of J. C. Edwards's terracotta production. The firm received many orders for the supply of red terracotta for commissions

Above: Detail of a Burmantofts faience panel on the exterior of Leicester railway station, showing two cherubs, one of whom is perched against the image of a steam locomotive. The station was rebuilt under the direction of the architect Charles Trubshaw in 1892.

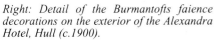

Left: The façade of the Punch Hotel, Hull (1896). All the intricate medieval-style architectural details and decorations have been carried out in Burmantofts terracotta.

Right: Detail of the Burmantofts faience decorations on the exterior of the Alexandra Hotel, Hull (c.1900).

Left: The head of a woman modelled in Burmantofts faience, part of the fountain in the entrance of the municipal baths in Ripon, North Yorkshire (1904).

The exterior of the Liberal Club, Infirmary Street, Leeds, by the architects Chorley & Connon (1890). J. C. Edwards made all the terracotta ornamentation.

such as the Eye, Ear and Throat Hospital (1879) in Shrewsbury, the Liberal Club (1890) and Metropole Hotel (1897–9) in Leeds, and the Victoria Law Courts (1891) in Birmingham. But there were other firms in the area, such as Henry Dennis and Henry R. Bowers. The latter supplied all the red terracotta for the Queen's School (1881–3) in Chester. So much terracotta was produced in Ruabon during the 1880s and 1890s that the town became known as 'Terracottapolis'.

A terracotta relief panel by J. C. Edwards on the exterior of Thomson Yates Laboratories, University of Liverpool (c.1890).

The terracotta statue of Queen Victoria on the exterior of the Queen's School, Chester, built in 1881-3. The terracotta was supplied by the firm of Henry R. Bowers, Ruabon, Wales.

If Doulton, Burmantofts and J. C. Edwards were the three biggest firms, there were also other suppliers throughout Britain, like Carter & Company in Poole, Dorset, the Hathern Station Brick & Terracotta Company in Hathern, Leicestershire, and Shaws of Darwen, Lancashire. In addition, there were other firms, including Minton, Hollins & Company, Maw & Company and Craven Dunnill, whose main production line was tiles but which also manufactured terracotta and faience

Detail of the façade of the County Constabulary, Ruabon, Wales, built in 1896. The terracotta name panel was probably made by J. C. Edwards.

when required. There were also small clay works that produced items for mainly local distribution, like the Clayton Fireclay Works of Clayton near Bradford. It produced the usual assortment of glazed bricks, sanitary pipes and chimney pots but also made ornamental salt-glazed terracotta building components like lintels, mullions and medallions, which can still be seen on late-Victorian houses in the area around Clayton.

Three small firms that occupy a special place in the history of terracotta and faience were the Della Robbia Pottery at Birkenhead, near Liverpool, the Medmenham Pottery at

Left: A faience fireplace surround by Maw & Company at the Gladstone Pottery Museum, Stoke-on-Trent (c.1870).

In the 1870s Maw & Company made faience roundels depicting the Four Seasons, of which Spring is shown here.

The interior of the Reading Room at Leeds Central Library, built in 1878–84, is extensively decorated with tiles and faience by E. Smith & Company, of Coalville, Leicestershire. The London artist Benjamin Creswick made the terracotta bust of Homer.

Marlow Common, Buckinghamshire, and the Compton Pottery, Compton, near Guildford. In contrast to the big firms with their mass output, these three were small, but their products were of a special artistic nature and strongly infused by current Arts and Crafts ideologies. The Della Robbia Pottery was in existence between 1894 and 1906. It was founded by Harold Steward Rathbone, a pupil of the Pre-Raphaelite painter Ford Madox Brown. Its pottery, tiles and architectural faience were modelled by hand from local clays and decorated with colourful faience glazes, which echoed strongly the products of the fifteenth-century Della Robbia workshop in Florence.

The Medmenham Pottery was also very much inspired by Italian polychrome faience work of the fifteenth century. Conrad Dressler, who had

Above: Decorative roof finials such as this terracotta dragon perched on a late-Victorian house in Headingley, Leeds, are an intriguing feature of domestic architecture of the period.

Left: A salt-glazed terracotta medallion with dancing cherubs on the exterior of The Elders, Brow Lane, Clayton, West Yorkshire, made by the nearby Clayton Fireclay Works (c.1895).

Left: A fountain made of polychrome faience by the Della Robbia Pottery in Birkenhead in 1899. It is now in the possession of the Museums and Art Galleries, Merseyside.

A faience capital with the head of a cow on the exterior of a former dairy in the High Street, Godalming, Surrey (c.1905).

27

The doorway of an idyllic cottage at Westfield Farm, Medmenham, Buckinghamshire, with a faience tympanum (c.1900) made by the local Medmenham Pottery and showing a man digging the soil.

previously worked for the Della Robbia Pottery in Birkenhead, set it up in 1897. One of its main commissions was the manufacture of a faience frieze and roundels for the Sunlight Chambers in Dublin in 1901, for the soap manufacturer Lord Leverhulme. These friezes were strongly

A faience tympanum depicting a sower above the doorway of a cottage at Westfield Farm, Medmenham, made by the Medmenham Pottery (c.1900).

A section of the polychrome frieze on the façade of the Sunlight Chambers, Dublin, built for the soap manufacturer Lord Leverhulme in 1901. The frieze was made by the Medmenham Pottery, Marlow Common, Buckinghamshire.

Detail of the façade of Ospedale del Ceppo, Pistoia, Italy (c.1525). The frieze in polychrome faience made by Santi Buglioni shows acts of charity, while the roundel by Giovanni della Robbia depicts the Annunciation to the Virgin. This kind of Italian polychrome ceramics exerted great influence on the Della Robbia Pottery in Birkenhead and the Medmenham Pottery at Marlow Common, Buckinghamshire.

influenced by Italian examples such as the magnificent early-sixteenth-century polychrome faience work on the exterior of Ospedale del Ceppo in Pistoia, Italy, made by the potters Giovanni della Robbia and Santi Buglioni.

An Arts and Crafts pottery rooted in local culture was established in Compton in 1895 under the direction of Mary Watts, the wife of the artist George Frederick Watts. When a new burial ground was opened in Compton she built a cemetery chapel (opened in 1898) for which, in the spirit of

The terracotta frieze depicting the Spirit of Love designed by Mary Watts on the exterior of the cemetery chapel, Compton, near Guildford (1895–8). The angels and Celtic decorations are imbued with mystical meanings.

29

A terracotta grave sculpture for an infant in the churchyard of St Nicholas's church, Peper Harow, Surrey. It is inscribed on the back with the words 'Made for my sweet Elizabeth by her loving mother April 1914'.

Below: Detail of the faience façade of the Beehive public house, Newcastle upon Tyne.

the Arts and Crafts Movement, local people using local red clay made all the terracotta under her guidance. The terracotta ornaments on the exterior of the chapel show strong influences of Celtic design. There are angels with long flowing hair, and complex patterns with interlacing knots. The whole pictorial scheme of the exterior of the chapel was imbued with a mixture of complex Christian symbolism and Celtic mysticism.

By the end of Queen Victoria's reign the use of functional and decorative terracotta and faience had become commonplace. Their application in buildings continued unabated in the Edwardian era. At the beginning of the twentieth century there was a notable shift from the use of unglazed terracotta to glazed faience for the exterior of buildings, as faience was

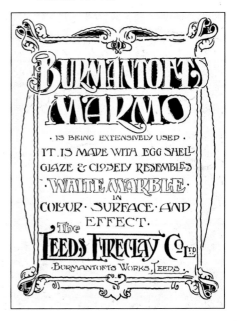

The White Horse Hotel, Aberystwyth, with a striking Edwardian faience exterior.

An advertisement for Burmantofts Marmo, c.1910.

more effective in resisting atmospheric pollution. This is clearly illustrated by Burmantofts, which in 1908 launched a new kind of faience, called Marmo, for exterior use in direct competition with Carraraware, developed earlier by Doulton. It was marketed as being 'made with egg shell glaze' and closely resembling 'white marble in colour, surface and effect'. If terracotta had at one time been marketed as 'artificial stone', faience material was now presented as a form of artificial marble. It seems that the competition with stone as a building material was never far from the manufacturer's mind.

During the Edwardian period neo-Baroque began to emerge as a favourite style for office blocks, pubs and shops. Façades were decorated with heavy-looking faience columns, capitals, tympanums, ornamental

Above left: A sculpture of the figure of Wisdom executed in Burmantofts Marmo on the exterior of the Scottish Union & National Insurance Company, Park Row, Leeds (1909). Thewlis & Company undertook the sculptural work.

Above right: A sculpture of the figure of Atlas executed in Burmantofts Marmo above the entrance of Atlas Chambers, King Street, Leeds (1910).

keystones and figurative sculpture. Edwardian pubs in particular were noted at that time for their use of colourful ceramic exteriors and interiors. This was the final flourish of Victorian ornament. However, much of this came to an end with the outbreak of the First World War in 1914. After the war new architectural ideas and practices emerged, which also affected the demand for architectural ceramics.

Contraction

Two main factors affected the production of architectural ceramics after the First World War. The first was economic contraction and the second was the emergence of Modernism in architecture and design. Modernist architects rejected the past, eschewed decoration and advocated the principle 'less is more'. Wall surfaces became plainer and there was less call for decorative features. Non-ceramic materials like glass, stone and concrete became prevalent. If faience material was used, it was mainly very plain and functional. This can be seen in the inter-war Odeon and Ritz cinema chains, and in department stores like Woolworths and Burton's. They show streamlined forms in combination with plain faience. Doulton's Carraraware, Burmantofts' two exterior faience products Marmo and Lefco, and Shaws' and Hathern's plain constructional faience were ideal for this purpose.

However, not everything became devoid of decoration. 'Egyptomania', which had spread through America and Europe after the discovery of Tutankhamun's tomb in 1922, also affected architectural design in Britain. It manifested itself particularly in cinema design, as can be seen in the former Carlton cinema (now a bingo hall), Essex Road, Islington, London (1930), designed by the cinema architect George Coles. It has a façade like an Egyptian temple, completely covered in faience with colourful friezes and columns made by Hathern.

Above: Detail of the decorations showing musical instruments on the exterior of the Majestic theatre (1922), City Square, Leeds, executed in Lefco by Burmantofts.

Left: The Modernist Odeon cinema in Sutton Coldfield, near Birmingham, with plain faience by Shaws of Darwen (1935).

Detail of the colourful Art Deco ceramics in a neo-Egyptian style on the façade of the Carlton cinema in Essex Road, Islington, London, designed by George Coles in 1930. Hathern made the polychrome faience.

Occasionally opportunities were afforded to sculptors like Frank Dobson and Gilbert Bayes to work in the medium of architectural ceramics. Frank Dobson was commissioned to enhance the façade of St Olave's House, Tooley Street, London. This is a Modernist office block completed in 1932 under the direction of the architect H. S. Goodhart Rendall. Dobson designed a series of remarkable semi-abstract ceramic relief sculptures made by Doulton for the central section of the façade above the main entrance.

The London sculptor Gilbert Bayes also favoured colourful faience sculpture as part of architecture. In the 1930s the St Pancras Housing Association built

The façade of St Olave's House, Tooley Street, London (1932). The Modernist ceramic relief sculptures were designed by Frank Dobson and made by Doulton in gilded stoneware on a black background.

the Sidney Street Estate in Camden, London. The architect I. Hamilton designed the scheme. He and Gilbert Bayes worked together to add colourful features to the estate in the form of ceramic lunettes depicting fairy tales above many windows, and little polychrome ceramic statues on washing-line posts which displayed themes that were linked to the names of the flats. St Michael's Flats, for example, had a central post with the archangel St Michael, and the smaller posts arranged around it in a circle had little statues of a devil. Doulton made all the ceramic decorations for this scheme in durable polychrome stoneware.

The great swan-song of this trend was the Doulton Building in London. In the late 1930s Doulton commissioned the architect T. P. Bennett to design a new

Right: A devil perched on a washing post at the St Michael's Flats, Camden, London, designed by the sculptor Gilbert Bayes and made by Doulton (1937).

Below: The Four Seasons clock designed by Gilbert Bayes and made by Doulton, Sidney Street Estate, Camden, London (1937).

35

Fishes on a washing post at St Anthony's Flats, Camden, London, designed by the sculptor Gilbert Bayes and made by Doulton (1937).

head office on the Albert Embankment. Completed in 1939, it had a severe block-like Modernist façade but, over the main entrance, room was made for a polychrome ceramic frieze showing 'Pottery Through the Ages', designed by Gilbert Bayes. The robust monumental handling of the form shows affinity with the formalist work of Bayes's contemporaries Eric Gill and Jacob Epstein. The building was demolished in the late 1970s but the frieze was rescued and is now in the Victoria and Albert Museum.

Although most architectural faience of the inter-war period was made by British firms there were also occasionally foreign suppliers, such as the firm of De Porceleyne Fles in Delft, Holland. In 1914–16 De Porceleyne Fles had supplied material for Holland House, in London, designed by the well-known Dutch architect H. P. Berlage, but it continued to export to Britain via Bell & Company in Northampton, which imported architectural faience for the façades of pubs, shops and offices.

Detail of the 'Pottery Through the Ages' frieze by Gilbert Bayes on Doulton House, Albert Embankment, London (1939). The building was demolished in the late 1970s, but the ceramic frieze was rescued and is now in the Victoria and Albert Museum.

Revival

The Modernist trend in architecture continued strongly after the Second World War, reaching its peak in the 1960s. In the 1970s new architectural ideas began to challenge the tenets of Modernism, first noticed in the writing and practice of the architect Robert Venturi. Buildings from the past were looked at again for inspiration and the use of ornamentation was re-examined. Terracotta and faience decorations on buildings made a comeback, like the brick and terracotta frieze on the exterior of the Potteries Museum in Hanley, Stoke-on-Trent, installed in 1980, and the terracotta decorations of flowers and birds on the exterior of the Cavern Walks shopping centre in Liverpool in 1985. Terracotta is also used in sculptural constructions, like the intriguing terracotta structure by David Hamilton in Blackett Street, Newcastle upon Tyne (1985), that hides a Metro ventilation shaft, and the terracotta bats on the 'Batley Bats' sculpture by Rory McNally erected in

A terracotta plaque with blue glaze on the exterior of Studio 10^1/2, a craft café in King Street, Hull (c.1970).

The architect David Backhouse used terracotta decorations made by Hathernware Ceramics on the exterior of the Cavern Walks shopping centre, Liverpool (1985). It was built on the site of the Cavern Club made famous by the Beatles; Cynthia Lennon, John Lennon's first wife, designed the terracotta motifs of roses and doves.

'Parson's Polygon', a decorative terracotta structure made by the sculptor David Hamilton in 1985. It conceals a ventilation shaft of the underground Metro in Blackett Street, Newcastle upon Tyne.

the centre of Batley, West Yorkshire, in 1995. The designs of new shopping malls can also include decorative terracotta. A good example is the Forum shopping centre in Chester built in 1995, where a series of attractive terracotta plaques made by Timothy Clapcott decorates the façade in Hamilton Place. The use of terracotta in the third millennium has been boosted by the new Art Gallery in Walsall built in 2000; the exterior of this striking Modernist building has been completely covered in terracotta tiles.

Another aspect of the revived interest in terracotta and faience has been the conservation and restoration of buildings. The large-scale demolition of Victorian and Edwardian buildings in many cities in the 1950s and 1960s began to abate in the 1970s. New ideas about retention, refurbishment and conservation of the architectural past resulted in the restoration of nineteenth- and early-twentieth-century buildings. Firms like Hathern and Shaws of Darwen became involved with the supply of material for restoration purposes. However, regaining lost skills took time. When the fabulous Victorian terracotta and

A terracotta plaque on the exterior of the Forum shopping centre, Hamilton Place, Chester, made by Timothy Clapcott in 1995.

Detail of a terracotta bat on the 'Batley Bats' sculpture, Hick Lane, Batley, West Yorkshire (1995). It was designed by the artist Rory McNally and made by Shaws of Darwen.

brick exterior of St Pauls House in Leeds was saved from demolition in the 1970s, decayed sections of the building could not be replaced with terracotta because the necessary manufacturing skills had been lost. Fibreglass components masquerading as terracotta were made instead. Yet by the time the Hackney Empire in London, dating from 1901, was restored in 1988 the required skills had been regained, and Shaws of Darwen made all replacements in appropriate faience material. This trend has gained momentum ever since, and matching replacement materials as well as expert advice on restoration and cleaning of terracotta and faience are now commonly available. Architectural ceramics in the form of terracotta and faience have once again become a prized addition to the architectural landscape of Britain, as part of restored buildings and new architectural schemes.

Further reading

Atterbury, Paul, and Irvine, Louise. *The Doulton Story*. Royal Doulton Tableware, 1979.
Barnard, Julian. *The Decorative Tradition*. The Architectural Press, 1973.
Garlick, Alan, et al. *Burmantofts Pottery*. Bradford Art Galleries & Museums and Leeds City Museums, 1983.
Girouard, Mark. *Alfred Waterhouse and the Natural History Museum*. British Museum (Natural History), 1981.
Hamilton, David. *Architectural Ceramics*. Thames & Hudson, 1978.
Kelly, Alison. *Mrs Coade's Stone*. The Self Publishing Association, 1990.
Stratton, Michael. 'Architectural Ceramics' in *Fired Earth: 1000 Years of Tiles in Europe*. Richard Dennis Publications and Tiles & Architectural Ceramics Society, 1991.
Stratton, Michael. *The Terracotta Revival*. Victor Gollancz, 1993.

Places to visit

British Museum, Great Russell Street, London WC1B 3DG.
 Telephone: 020 7323 8838. Website: www.britishmuseum.org
Gladstone Pottery Museum, Uttoxeter Road, Longton, Stoke-on-Trent, Staffordshire ST3 1PQ. Telephone: 01782 234567. Website: www.stoke.gov.uk
Jackfield Tile Museum, Ironbridge Gorge, Telford, Shropshire TF8 7LJ (part of Ironbridge Gorge Museum). Telephone: 01952 433424. Website: www.ironbridge.org.uk
Victoria and Albert Museum, Cromwell Road, South Kensington, London SW7 2RL. Telephone: 020 7942 2000. Website: www.vam.ac.uk

The Tiles and Architectural Ceramics Society: Membership enquiries to TACS Membership Secretary, 27 Spurn Lane, Holden Smithy, Diggle, Oldham, OL3 5QP. Website: www.tilesoc.org.uk

The top section of the Turkey Café, Granby Street, Leicester (1900–1), executed in coloured Carraraware by Doulton.